American Furniture
of the Colonial Period

American Furniture
of the Colonial Period

MARVIN D. SCHWARTZ

The Metropolitan Museum of Art

Printed in Verona, Italy, by Mondadori Publishing Company, Inc.
Type set by Custom Composition Company, Inc., York, Pennsylvania
Designed by Peter Oldenburg

ACKNOWLEDGMENTS

Cooperation and advice from the American Wing staff were essential to the writing of this study, and Frances Gruber, Morrison H. Heckscher, and the Curator in Charge of the Wing, Berry B. Tracy, were gracious consultants who made innumerable improvements to the manuscript.

LIBRARY OF CONGRESS CATALOGING IN PUBLICATION DATA

New York (City). Metropolitan Museum of Art. American
  furniture of the colonial period.

  Bibliography: p.
  1. Furniture, Colonial—United States—Catalogs. 2. Furniture—United States—Catalogs. 3. New York (City). Metropolitan Museum of Art.
I. Schwartz, Marvin D. II. Title.

NK2406.N37 1976   749.2'14'07401471   76-18763
ISBN 0-87099-149-3

Contents

Introduction

American colonial furniture is prized today not only for its appearance but also for its associations, not so much with famous men and historic places, but with the daily lives and habits of our ancestors. From the straight lines of simple oak tables and chairs of the 1600s to the elaborate curves of high chests made on the eve of the Revolution, colonial furniture illustrates America's evolution from settlement to nation. The independent spirit that determined the politics of the New World was reflected in the aesthetic approach of its craftsmen; no matter what innovation fashion dictated to England or the Continent, the American furniture maker chose only what he admired, combining stylish features with old-fashioned ones to produce furniture that, at its best, is handsome, well made, and restrained in design.

Since American design was mainly inspired by British models, distinguishing American work from the British can often be difficult. But, while English craftsmen were sometimes enthusiastic in the application of ornament to the detriment of the design or strength of a piece, American furniture is consistently sturdy—solidly constructed and free of fragile decoration. When one recent Metropolitan Museum acquisition, a chair from a set made just before the Revolution, was originally offered for sale in England, connoisseurs recognized it as uncharacteristic of English work. By careful scrutiny of the carving,

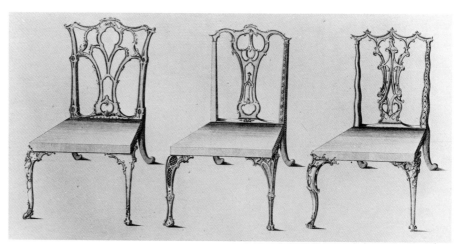

Fig. 1 Plate XV from *The Gentleman and Cabinet-Maker's Director* by Thomas Chippendale (London, 1754), Museum Purchase

an American expert was able to attribute the chair to a Philadelphia cabinet-maker, Benjamin Randolph. Randolph followed the same basic pattern of the English models, but he cut his designs thicker, avoiding the risks of flimsy construction. Comparisons of engravings of chairs (Fig. 1) in *The Gentleman and Cabinet-Maker's Director,* the pattern book by the English furniture maker Thomas Chippendale, with actual chairs inspired by them (Fig. 2) also show that the American was less faithful in copying motifs than the English craftsman, nearly always making his work more solid than it appeared in the illustration.

American design has sometimes been separated into two categories, urban and rural, but this distinction works better in theory than in practice. As a rule, however, "city" craftsmen usually adapted the ambitious efforts of London, or even of York or Dublin, keeping fairly close to the original designs. The "country" cabinetmaker, in contrast, worked with designs that could be executed quickly, usually choosing forms with a minimum of embellishment.

Fig. 2 Mahogany chair in Chippendale style, Boston or Salem, Massachusetts, about 1765–1770, H. 38⅝ in., 39.88.2, Gift of Mrs. Paul Moore, 1939

His carving was schematic and simplified, stressing economy of line but with enough ingenuity to create attractive pieces.

Although the issue is still in controversy, many experts believe that a number of characteristics, in construction as well as in decoration, can be associated with specific colonies. The range of embellishment, richness of detail, chicness by London standards, and the connection with English models is wide within colonial furniture, but at each center of cabinetmaking the designs were consistent. Delicate dovetailing and grooved edges on the tops of drawer sides, for example, are found on eighteenth-century Massachusetts pieces with small-scale, elegant carving, while Connecticut pieces with a more schematic rendering of decorative detail have rougher interiors. Boston cabinetmakers followed the elegant trends in London more closely than did their counterparts in Newport or Philadelphia. Philadelphia produced the most ornate furniture. New York cabinetmakers tended to favor heavier proportions, resulting in furniture with the appearance of strength. Charleston products are often easiest to confuse with London wares, but other Southern furniture is relatively plain.

The identification of local elements of a design can often provide the origins of an example. By examining claw-and-ball feet, it is often possible to confirm a provenance suggested by other features. New England claw-and-ball feet (Fig. 3) are cut so that the claws appear to grasp the ball tightly. One type of New York example is more stylized, with what looks like a taller foot carved in a pattern in which the "knuckles" form the corners of a square (Fig. 4). The rear talon is straight on this type, while on most others it curves around the ball. Another kind of New York claw-and-ball foot resembles Philadelphia examples, which tend to be squat, with well-defined claws on flattened balls (Fig. 5).

Investigations into regional differences also consider the kinds of woods used in furniture making. Although the surface wood in the major centers is dependent upon style, the secondary woods, used for such interior features as corner blocks and drawer linings, were of local origin.

The chronological sequence applied to American colonial furniture is not completely documented, in part because furniture makers in different regions did not always alter their styles at the same moment, but most experts agree on the basic periods. The earliest American furniture to have survived to the present day appears to have been made in the 1650s and is now called Pilgrim style. In London by 1640, oak had been replaced by walnut and walnut veneers on other woods, but the earliest American work was produced in oak, not in the latest London fashion, but in the style of the late Renaissance. The heavy, paneled chairs, tables, and cupboards made in the early American settlements resemble English furniture of the sixteenth and early seventeenth centuries. As time went on, American furniture became closer in style to contemporary English models. Proportions began to lighten by the turn of the century;

furniture adopted more architectural lines, with legs turned in columnar patterns. This style, inspired by the fashionable style of the seventeenth century, often called the baroque, is known by furniture connoisseurs as the William and Mary. With the change in design, small tables and small chests of drawers were added to the repertory. Styles changed again in 1730, bringing the Queen Anne with its additional furniture forms, including round and rectangular tea tables. Lines became organic, rather than architectural, most

Fig. 3 New England type claw-and-ball foot
Fig. 4 New York type claw-and-ball foot
Fig. 5 Philadelphia type claw-and-ball foot

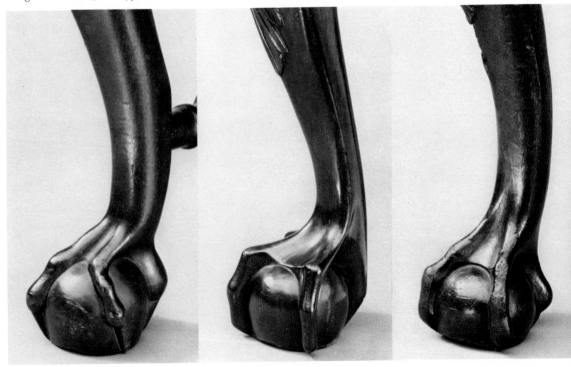

evident in the outward curving knee of the cabriole leg. The relative simplicity of veneers and decoration of the Queen Anne was succeeded by the more ornate carving of the last colonial style, the Chippendale, in about 1760.

FURNITURE MAKING

The furniture maker of the colonial period was known first as a joiner, and later as a cabinetmaker, although the terms were sometimes used interchangeably. As defined in *Mechanick Exercises*, a seventeenth-century English manual by Joseph Moxon, "Joynery is an Art Manual whereby several pieces of Wood are so fitted and joyned together by straight lines, squares, Miters or any Bevel, that they shall seem one entire piece." The joiner specialized in putting together wooden objects, buildings, and boats by the mortise-and-tenon method of construction. The word "cabinetmaker," coming into common use in the colonies only after 1700, designated a craftsman who concentrated in the making of "case" furniture, or chests and cupboards, using more intricate techniques, including dovetailing, inlay, and veneering. Advertisements of the period also mention chairmakers, although several who listed themselves as such are known to have also made case pieces. Even after cabinetmakers were well established as the furniture makers for colonial America, the term joiner was still applied to some craftsmen working outside of the large centers. For example, Thomas Burling of New York, who advertised himself as a cabinet- and chairmaker, offered "all kinds of stuff" to "country joiners." Account books from colonial shops add to the confusion by recording that even the most fashionable cabinetmakers produced coffins and rustic furniture as well as fine pieces. Whatever he was called, the maker was also the seller of his furniture. His stock, augmented by goods imported from England, was distributed directly from his shop, without the assistance of middlemen. Advertisements indicate that furniture was made mostly on speculation, but commissions were apparently accepted from patrons with special demands.

Few documents record the number of workers employed in American shops. Traditionally, the maker had the assistance of apprentices, just learning the trade, and journeymen, who had achieved the skills necessary to produce fine work. The average establishment probably employed less than ten craftsmen. London shops sometimes rostered over a hundred men. Americans often commissioned services of specialists for fine carving, sometimes in exchange for furniture wood or finished furniture.

The methods and tools used by house carpenters, joiners, and turners are explained in *Mechanick Exercises*. In seventeenth-century England, each of these craftsmen belonged to a separate guild with its own distinct privileges and obligations. Carpenters often acted as supervising contractors, assigning work to the appropriate specialist. In the colonies, the distinction between the types of woodworkers was not as rigidly observed. According to Moxon, the joiner concentrated on, among other things, the paneling of rooms and production of furniture, while the carpenter constructed the basic framework of the house. The turner used a lathe to turn or spin narrow rods or planks of wood into such objects as chair legs, arms, and stretchers, and stair railings. Other materials, including ivory and brass, were turned for applied ornaments and miniature columns and railings.

The tools illustrated in *Mechanick Exercises* for the joiner's use include planes, saws, drills, hammers, mallets, chisels, and devices to keep edges straight (Fig. 6). Whether he was making a wall or a chest, the joiner was advised to use the mortise-and-tenon technique. A frame was made by fitting the tenons, or projecting ends of planks, into mortises, or slots in the connecting planks. Pegs were used to reinforce the construction, and Moxon recom-

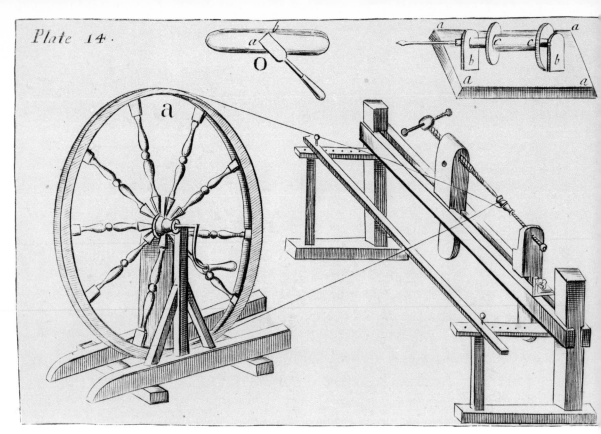

Fig. 6 Plate 14 from *Mechanick Exercises* by Joseph Moxon (London, 1683), Rogers Fund, Library. Shown from left to right are: at top, a gauge to smooth irregularities and a drill on a drill bench; at bottom, a great wheel turned with handles and a lathe with object being turned on it

mended strengthening the bonds with glue. Into this frame, the joiner installed thinner boards, planed at the ends to fit into grooves in the framing planks. Drawers, when they were used, were made by overlapping the two sides and nailing them together. A groove in the drawer sides would be fitted to runners made of strips of wood and nailed to the insides of the chest.

In the "Art of Turning," Moxon lists the types of lathes and advises on the methods of cutting planks into the architectural-type decoration sometimes applied to seventeenth-century furniture. Feet, which were occasionally added to chests or cupboards, were turned in flat turnip or oval melon shapes. Turned decoration was done in maple, hickory, pine, and a few other woods and was sometimes stained a reddish walnut color or painted black in imitation of ebony, then popular in Europe.

With the introduction of the William and Mary style toward the end of the seventeenth century, the simple art of joinery was supplanted by cabinet-making, and function became subordinate to design. The elegance of the new style required concealing construction and emphasizing ornament. Finer woods, a greater variety of decorative motifs, and special surface treatments were introduced. Thin layers of finely grained wood were glued to furniture carcasses in the technique known as veneering. In the construction of case furniture, dovetailing replaced the mortise-and-tenon method, its interlacing, dovetail-shaped tenons making possible thinner, lighter proportions. After 1700 the furniture maker dropped his role of all-around woodworker and became a specialist.

The furniture of the Queen Anne and Chippendale styles required ever more time-consuming, specialized work. More hardwoods were used, especially walnut and mahogany, and they were used extravagantly in the execution of such forms as the cabriole leg. By the last half of the eighteenth century, the colonies were prosperous, and the patrons of American furniture makers could afford to pay for these less economical, but more elaborate and more fashionable designs.

Early or late, simple or elaborate, the surviving colonial furniture is the work of skilled craftsmen. Even the most ordinary, utilitarian chest of the seventeenth century reveals subtle refinements in construction and design. While less affluent colonists continued to make and use plain furniture with simple, turned legs—usually of pine—throughout the eighteenth century, the crudely made amateurish pieces sometimes seen today almost always prove to be later work, often the pioneer efforts of the nineteenth century.

Except for the skill exhibited in his work, however, little is known about the American cabinetmaker. Account books offer some information about the kind of output and patronage, but details about the personalities and lifestyles of America's earliest furniture makers have not been uncovered. Only the fine craftsmanship and unique vitality of their work survives, a legacy that tantalizes us with the mystery as well as the beauty of its creation.

American Furniture
of the Colonial Period

The Seventeenth-century, or Pilgrim, Style

The heavy proportions and simple lines of Pilgrim-style furniture were apparently popular in all of the seaboard colonies, but more is known about New England examples than those of any other area. This early furniture is usually made of oak in bold designs that appear to combine functionalism with classic lines. The designs relate most closely to contemporary English country models, and both American and provincial English furniture of the seventeenth-century relate to models produced in London in the sixteenth century. Made by the techniques of the joiner with the addition of turned and carved elements, the furniture appears massive and plain, composed of straight lines and severely squared corners. The joiner emphasized solidity; decoration, whether carved into solid panels or applied in the form of turned spindles, was secondary.

Oak was the logical choice of wood—hard, able to withstand temperature changes, insects, and heavy use. In Europe, oak was used for the best furniture throughout the Middle Ages, when decoration seemed less important than utility. More elaborate furniture designs with intricate carving were introduced with the advent of the High Renaissance in Italy, about 1500, and spread throughout Europe by about 1600. Oak was then replaced by walnut, a wood that is more handsomely grained and easier to carve. While American craftsmen chose to use some of the fashionable elements of European design, they

continued to produce most of their work in oak and pine until the end of the seventeenth century, modifying motifs to reduce the amount of carving. As a concession to fashion, however, they often stained the finished surface a reddish brown to simulate walnut, evidence that Americans were aware of Old World trends even if they were not following them. Ebony borders with decorative panels on English examples were translated by the Americans as applied corbels, dentils, spindles, and bosses in maple or hickory painted black.

The characteristic seventeenth-century room in the colonies was quite plain. Walls were rough plaster or vertical pine boards. The ceiling revealed the major oak supporting beams, and the floors were formed from wide planks of pine, stained walnut or simply sanded and left unfinished. Small leaded glass casement windows were set in simple oak or pine frames. This modest interior, with its variety of textures, was complemented by a few large pieces of furniture that were restricted in both type and design.

For storage the early settler usually had an ordinary chest, now called a blanket chest, which had a bottom, four sides, and a lid, usually hinged at the back. Occasionally a drawer or two was added under the storage area. Drawers had been used for several centuries in Italy, but chests of drawers seem to have been rare in the colonies before the eighteenth century. A smaller storage form consisting of a box that opened from the top and was set on a stand of high legs may have been a bookstand or a washstand. The flat or slant-topped "Bible" box was also used for storage. Placed on a chest or table, it could serve as a book support or writing table. Another small form that was placed on a chest or table is the chest with doors that conceal tiers of small drawers. This small cabinet was used to store valuables like spices or jewels. The largest and most ambitious forms by the American furniture makers are the court and press cupboards. Both pieces have open shelf space; the court cupboard is enclosed only at the top, while the press cupboard has both upper and lower enclosed areas.

Tables were a necessity in even the most sparsely furnished room. Although few seventeenth-century tables have survived, several types are known: trestle forms, rectangular examples with boldly turned legs, small tables that might double as stools, and a few variants with folding or drop-leaf tops. Their age can frequently be gauged by the proportions or size of the turnings, since the turnings of legs and stretchers are thought to have become increasingly lighter and smaller.

The chair is the form least likely to be made of oak. Seventeenth-century examples are mostly in maple, ash, or nut woods, which are easier to turn than oak. The typical example is thronelike: large, formal, and designed for erect posture rather than a comfortable slouch. One theory for the severity and size of this chair is that it was reserved for the head of the family and honored guests. Other family members sat on stools when dining or working.

In spite of the plain look of seventeenth-century furniture, it is finely constructed. Each board has been carefully cut and planed; the mortise-and-tenon joints are snug; edges are embellished with handsomely profiled classical moldings; and surfaces are smoothed and stained. Although ornaments are often so schematic that they hardly relate to their classical models, they are rendered with finesse. The heaviness of the proportions makes seventeenth-century pieces seem more massive than they actually are. Although chairs are wider and taller than fine eighteenth-century examples, chests are often no more than five feet long. The court cupboard, which seems the largest of the early pieces, is never as much as five feet high, in contrast to the eight- and nine-foot chests of the late eighteenth century.

The form of a chair often provides the best insight into the characteristics of a style. Although basically functional, the seventeenth-century chair was also

1. *Turned-post armchair* **2.** *Ladderback armchair*

a major decorative element in the typical stark interior of the period. The turned-post chair (1) is a design that can be traced to at least the eleventh century, when it was used as the throne in representations of the Virgin Mary. Many colonial turned-post chairs have survived. This one has typical turnings; legs, arms, back, and stretchers are all decorated with rings and urn shapes. However, the rear posts are unusually angled and in two sections rather than in the standard single straight post. Each element is generously proportioned—large and full—and the seat is woven of appropriately rough rush. The example

6

descended in the family of a seventeenth-century resident of New York before coming to the Metropolitan Museum.

The use of turned posts for the legs and arm supports and a set of slats for the back represents a refinement in the design of American chairs (2). The shape of the slats was inspired by pediment scrolls, a popular architectural motif of the baroque style. The arrangement of the slats in a ladder pattern was introduced in the seventeenth century and was used throughout the eighteenth century. In later examples, the posts and slats were lighter and thinner. This is one of a group of chairs that has been associated with New England.

More peculiar to the seventeenth century is the chair made of solid panels, the wainscot chair (3). The design of this chair is more complex than that of

3. *Wainscot armchair*

4. *Chair-table*

most American examples, and some connoisseurs speculate that the chair may actually be English or that its embellishments may have been added during an early restoration. It looks more elaborate than the turned-post examples but actually involved no more labor. The technique of the turner has been exchanged for that of the joiner. The fantastic dragonlike creatures carved at the top look as though they might have been borrowed from the gravestone carver's repertory, but the rosettes and meanders on the borders are classical motifs, and the panels of flowers appear to have been inspired by a Middle Eastern tree-of-life pattern seen on contemporary textiles. The chair is one of the more elaborate versions of the wainscot design, with unusually rich detail on the arm supports and front legs.

The back of the chair-table (4) flips down to form a table or stands vertically to make a chair, which can then be placed against the wall. The form was so popular that examples are known from the seventeenth century until the

8

1800s. Chair-tables were mentioned in inventories of sixteenth-century England and in America as early as the 1650s. Signs of seventeenth-century origin on this piece include the heaviness of the turned legs, the crisp contours of the moldings, and the grooves in the skirt and in the stretchers. Later examples are generally much plainer. The turnings resemble those on the simpler wainscot chairs. Oak was used for the base, pine for the top.

The upholstered chair without arms (5) has been called a Cromwellian after the famous Republican and a farthingale after a dress with a wide skirt that made chairs without arms a necessity. The form was popular on both sides of the Atlantic in the seventeenth century. According to tradition, the Museum's example was once owned by the founder of Rhode Island, Roger Williams. The turnings are cut in the ball pattern, and the piece resembles an example known to have been made in Connecticut. The upholstery is original—an American interpretation of the geometric design needlework known as "Turkey work" after the "Turkey carpet" pile technique on which it was based.

5. *Cromwellian,*
or farthingale,
upholstered chair

9

6. *Blanket chest attributed to Thomas Dennis*

The blanket chest (6)—a rectangular box topped by a lid—was used for storage in the ancient as well as the modern world. Most chests in colonial America were plain. Elaborate examples like this one were decorated to suit current taste. The carving is typical of seventeenth-century style. Across the upper border is a stylized rosette pattern; on the sides are leaves. The outer front panels are carved in the tree-of-life motif and the center one in the design of a tulip. Both designs were probably inspired by Near Eastern decorative treatments, which had become fashionable in England and in the New World. The motifs are also found on English models, but the carving on American examples tends to be simpler and more stylized, an adaptation for the oak grain. The leaf and flower motifs of this chest are rendered flatter than the Old World versions but in a complex pattern that retains the essence of the originals. This example has traditionally been attributed to Thomas Dennis, an

10

Ipswich, Massachusetts, craftsman who has been credited with some of the finest and most intricately carved furniture made in seventeenth-century Massachusetts. Recent studies have shown, however, that Dennis was probably not the only craftsman working in the style that has been associated with his name.

At the same time that Dennis and his colleagues were producing pieces with consistently complex decoration, other craftsmen working in New England were carving with much less concern for the precise duplication of classical details. The carving of 7 is more schematic and less detailed than that of 6, although the spirit is similar. Despite the seeming roughness of the carving, the joinery reveals the maker's advanced knowledge of his craft. The initials on the lid detail a family genealogy, probably carved in 1910, the last date given. The long narrow marks on the lid were left by eighteenth-century hinges, removed when the piece was restored.

7. *Blanket chest*

8. *Two-drawer Wethersfield chest*

9. *Hadley chest*

The name Wethersfield has been applied to this type of two-drawer chest with a combination of floral carving and applied ornament as embellishment (8). On typical examples the three panels at the top are carved in low relief with stylized tulip and sunflower motifs. This example repeats the tulip on the center panel and bears the initials of the original owner. Such carving is used with minor variations on a number of chests that have been found in the neighborhood of Wethersfield and Hartford, Connecticut. The ebonized spindles, which are based on architectural motifs, add color and surface interest.

A number of stylistically similar dower chests of the late seventeenth century and early eighteenth century are often called Hadley chests after the town in Massachusetts near which many of them were made (9). Over forty have been associated, through their carved initials, with young ladies of marriageable age, living between Hartford, Connecticut, and Deerfield, Massachusetts, when the chests were made. Here, the carved ornament is flatter and more schematic than on 6 or 8. Although the same technique of rendering flowers in relief by cutting away the background has been used here, the result is more abstract and more naive than on 8. The carver has emphasized the outline of the pattern without concern for perspective or realism, but in so doing has produced a piece with an almost calligraphic vitality.

The painted chest (10), dated 1708, was made by the same mortise-and-tenon construction as 9, but the ornament is more in the style of the eighteenth century. Within the framework of grooved stiles and rails is a floral decoration on a background that resembles the lacquerlike surface produced by the painting technique called "japanning," which was popular, particularly in Connecticut, until about 1730. The thistle and rose in the upper panels are not oriental, however, but were Stuart symbols employed by partisans of the Catholic pretender to the British crown. The motifs also appear on a number of

10. *Painted chest with drawer*

chests in the William and Mary style. This example is a curious one, since it is conservative in form but advanced in decorative treatment.

The painted decoration of 11 is typical for the seventeenth century. The motifs are picked out in bold, heavy lines in relief, while in the eighteenth century they are executed with more delicacy and less clarity. Chests of drawers are rare for the period, but this one can be distinguished from later versions by the thickness of the detail. The sides are made of stiles and rails enclosing a center panel, joined by mortise-and-tenon construction. The solid drawer fronts are decorated with a frame of applied moldings that are painted with a grain to suggest walnut. The floral pattern of the center panels resembles that of 10. The heavy overall proportions, the ball feet, the thick moldings at the bottom and top of the piece, the color, and the graining are standard seventeenth-century features. Examples of this type have been associated with Massachusetts.

11. *Painted chest with drawers*

The name "court cupboard" (12) has been given to this kind of display piece. The top, the lower shelf, and often the ledge in front of the enclosed area were used to display ceramics, pewter, silver, or other decorative objects. The court cupboard was first known in sixteenth-century England. It was out of fashion in London by the mid-seventeenth century but was still produced in rural areas of England and in the colonies through the early eighteenth century. This example has been attributed to Connecticut craftsmen; it is smaller and less elaborate than many Massachusetts examples. The legs and supports for the upper shelf are turned in a bulbous vase and ring pattern that is a variation on an important baroque motif, the spiral design. The classical elements—the corbels on the cornice and the molding framing parts of the piece—are characteristic for such cupboards.

A cupboard with an enclosed lower section is called a press cupboard (13). The flat carving on the cornice and on the center drawer identifies this example as one of a group of pieces that has been traced to seventeenth-century New Haven Colony ownership. Traces of black paint on the applied bosses, spin-

12. *Court cupboard*   **13.** *Press cupboard*

dles, and turned columns show that these embellishments were originally ebonized. The carved decoration consists of two variations of classical frieze patterns, both flat and stylized but less abstract than the decoration on 8 or 9.

The most sophisticated examples of seventeenth-century cupboards have been attributed to the area of Plymouth County, Massachusetts. This press cupboard (14) has the kind of decoration seen on several cupboards from Plymouth. The concept of design is more subtle than that of 13. Drawers, a sign of an advance in form, replace the doors in the lower section. The use of serrated, or dog-tooth moldings on the borders, the patterns of moldings on the doors of the upper storage area, and the spindles applied at either side to suggest pilasters are evidence of the expert ability of the craftsman.

This small chest with a set of drawers enclosed by a door served as a jewel or spice box (15). The side panels are carved in a stylized floral pattern, while the door is decorated with moldings arranged in an octagonal pattern and applied spindles like those on 14. Small pieces such as this, made to be set on tables or chests, follow the basic design of larger storage pieces.

14. *Plymouth County press cupboard*   **15.** *Spice or jewel box*

16. *Trestle table*

17. *Gateleg folding table*

18

The trestle table (16), with its narrow top and braced legs, is a form that originated in the Middle Ages. The design is a particularly practical one, since the table can easily be dismantled for moving and storage. While the form varied little from century to century, this example can be identified as a seventeenth-century piece from its chamfered posts.

This gateleg folding table (17) is a curious mixture of early and late elements. The basic form was known in England in the early seventeenth century, but by the late seventeenth century it was more commonly interpreted with thin legs and rich veneers. The turned legs and applied spindles of this example are characteristic of seventeenth-century forms. The tortoiseshell pattern of the painted surface is not original, although its colors of red and black were used in the period. No table identical to this one in both proportion and surface treatment has yet been discovered.

Many rectangular tables with turned legs are known from the eighteenth century, but few seventeenth-century examples have survived. The design of 18 is typical of the seventeenth century: the turnings are bold, the details simple, and the top is almost square, a shape rarely encountered on later tables of this type.

18. *Rectangular table*

19. *Joint stool*

"Joint stool" is the popular name for this basic piece of seating furniture, which may also have served as a table (19). "Joint" refers to the joining technique used to make these stools. The type of turnings on the legs is an accurate indication of both period and quality. Fine examples have handsome turnings in the heavy proportions that characterize seventeenth-century fashion.

Skillful joinery is also evident in this cradle (20). Like the blanket chests, the

20. *Cradle*

piece was constructed as a plain box made of a frame filled with solid panels. The seventeenth-century origins of the piece are suggested by the grooved boards and the heavy finials.

The box-on-frame with a drawer (21) may have been used to store either toilet articles or books. A number of examples of the form have survived, but no conclusive evidence concerning its use has been found. Regardless of its function, the piece is representative of seventeenth-century joinery. The decoration resembles that of other forms, but the ball turnings are a particularly unusual detail for this kind of piece.

21. *Box-on-frame with drawer*

William and Mary Style

1690–1730

Whereas earlier furniture makers had often used classical motifs as decoration, the cabinetmaker of the William and Mary period based his designs on an interpretation of the ideals of classical beauty, creating pieces that were first to be admired, then to be used. Columns, scrolls, urns, and panels bordered with moldings were rendered in the spirit of the baroque, the international style that dominated European design in the mid-seventeenth century. In contrast to the precision and balance of Renaissance art and architecture, the baroque offered a freedom of design and movement within the repertory of classical motifs. As before, American furniture makers adapted the fashions of England to suit New World taste. "William and Mary" is in fact only a term of convenience for this style, which combined design features popular during the reign, from 1690 to 1701, of the British king and queen with features of earlier and later periods. Although the relationship is probably coincidental, the name of the Dutch-born king calls attention to the "Dutch" features of the style, such as the elaborate veneers and marquetry that adorned both the English models and their American counterparts. While American furniture makers continued to blend whatever elements they found pleasing, whether conservative or fashionable, the William and Mary period shows them to be at least in stride with the major trends of the time.

Such sophistication in furniture styles would have been impossible without

22

social change. About 1690, American towns began to develop from small communities struggling for survival into urban centers with schools and stylish houses that rivaled the achievements of English cities. The plain, almost purely functional style of architecture, with its exposed beams and rough plaster walls, yielded to a style in which pilasters and columns offered elegance, if no actual support. Paneling was cut in patterns reminiscent of those on walls of Italian Renaissance villas. In furniture, the benefit of the new affluence was that homeowners could afford the labor and expensive materials required to produce fine work in the most fashionable style. Cabinetmakers, with their time-consuming techniques of dovetailing and veneering, replaced joiners and added refinement to the American furniture-making tradition. With the change in taste, craftsmen discarded coarse-textured oak for smoother, richly grained walnut, often applied in veneers to obtain the most exciting patterns. Another kind of surface treatment that enjoyed increased popularity was japanning, a technique that attempted to simulate the appearance of Japanese and Chinese lacquer with layers of varnish and paint. To conceal details of construction, half-round moldings were nailed over side joints and drawer edges. Tops of chests were crowned with cornices, and some high chests were given deep crowns that accommodate a convex or concave frieze. The division between the upper and lower sections of high chests were decorated with heavy curved moldings. Standard baroque designs, such as scroll, spiral, or trumpet-shaped legs, were adapted from designs popular on the Continent earlier in the seventeenth century. Skirts on high chests and tables and stretchers were made of thin boards in curving lines. Ball feet were screwed into the turned legs after stretchers had been set in place, making pieces easy to dismantle and move. Scrolled, fluted, and curved "Spanish" feet were an alternate design, carved on other turned legs. Even interior fittings, such as drawer sides, were light, delicate, and carefully made.

24

Chair construction was still simple, but the appearance of chairs had changed. Since the size and function of a chair is more or less determined by human anatomy, the form would seem to offer little possibility for innovation. Exactly the opposite is the case: it is the chair, more than any other form of American furniture, that expresses the essence of a particular style. While the proportions of this William and Mary chair (22) are as solid and heavy as those of earlier chairs, the impression is strikingly different. The elegant, high-relief carving of the leaf and scroll ornament on the back and stretchers is set off by the simplicity of the turned legs, arm supports, and stiles. The effort is typical of flamboyant work of the beginning of the eighteenth century, when a few basic motifs were artfully employed to achieve an impression of grandeur. Leather upholstery was characteristic for the period; "leather chairs" were mentioned in a number of early New England listings. This chair was probably made in New England.

The side chair (23) clearly resembles 22. The carved top rail flanked by

22. *Armchair*

23. *Side chair*

turned stiles and the leather back are similar, but the front stretcher is in a ball pattern. The ball turning became a standard feature on chairs and was used until about 1800. Here, the scroll and leaf motifs are compressed and more deeply cut to suit the narrow proportions and tall back that are typical of William and Mary side chairs. Not as impressively ornamented as armchairs, side chairs of the period are equally monumental and equally baroque in spirit. This example has traditionally been considered a product of New York.

Split balusters with flat sides to the front, another baroque-inspired design, compose the back of this chair (24). The techniques of carving and turning are again combined. The classical shape of the balusters is an ideal complement to

24. *Baluster side chair*

25. *Butterfly table*

the scroll and leaf design on the top rail. The front feet are carved in the fluted scroll design called Spanish, seen almost exclusively on William and Mary furniture, while the front and side stretchers are turned in the popular ball pattern, also seen on 23. These simple elements add elegance to the overall design, but its utilitarian character is revealed by the rush seat, shown covered with a cushion. Rush was popular as a material for chair seats from the late seventeenth until the late nineteenth centuries, but after 1730 it was almost always used only for the plain furniture now generally considered to be of country origin. The chair may have been made in New England.

The butterfly table is so named for the shape of the brackets that swing out from the base to support its leaves. 25 is a typical example, although the type has many variations. Splayed legs and stretchers turned in the double-vase pattern, characteristic of the early eighteenth century, form a solid rectangular frame. When open, the top forms an oval, the standard shape for finer examples of butterfly tables. The scalloped edges of the supports also testify to the high quality of the work on this fairly simple form. The maple wood and delicate proportions of the turnings suggest that it was made in New England.

This oval-topped table with splayed legs (26) is one of the many types of small tables made during the William and Mary period. The table is small enough to have been used as one of a group in a public room, so it is often called a tavern table, but such small tables were also popular in homes in the early eighteenth century as tea, writing, or work tables. In fact, the table is probably too subtle in design for tavern use. The scrolled Spanish feet are neatly complemented by the grooved borders of the stretchers and the complex double arches on the skirt. The vase shapes on the turnings of the splayed legs are particularly graceful.

26. *Oval-topped table with splayed legs*

27. *Gateleg table*

Another popular form of small table (27) has a trestle base with gatelegs that can be pulled out to support the folding leaves of the top. When the legs are pushed back against the base, the piece becomes a narrow stand that can be put out of the way. The delicate double-vase turnings on the legs and the curves of the feet of the center trestle make a simple table elegant.

The large gateleg table with turned legs was another popular form of the eighteenth century (28). Few American houses of the period had dining rooms, and a table that could be converted from a dining table to a small table was a necessity. The turnings of the legs on this table are urn-shaped, a feature that has been associated with New England makers. The stretchers are turned in the ball design, also seen on chairs (23, 24). The dovetailed joints, visible inside the

28. *Large gateleg table*

29. *Blanket chest with drawer*

drawer, are a characteristic detail of early eighteenth-century cabinetmaking.

The traditional blanket chest of the seventeenth century was updated when the William and Mary style came into fashion by the addition of lively details such as decorative moldings and painted designs. 29 is made of pine instead of oak and is therefore thinner and lighter than its seventeenth-century predecessors. The absence of any embellishment in relief, except for a molding around the base and over the drawer, also emphasizes the lightness of form. The elegance of the piece is in the painted decoration. The floral pattern on a

30. *High chest*

reddish brown ground appears on many japanned chests. The ground is probably inspired by oriental red lacquer, and the patterns follow suggestions published late in the seventeenth century. The chest is one of a group of simple forms associated with craftsmen active in Guilford, Connecticut, between 1700 and 1730.

The high chest (30), now generally known as a highboy, is in two parts: a stand with drawers supporting a chest of drawers. The form was popular during most of the eighteenth century. The earliest examples, like this one, closely resemble English models, which have trumpet-turned legs with inverted cups. While the high chest all but disappeared in England after 1740, Americans continued to make versions in later styles, substituting curved cabriole legs for turned ones. Detail for detail, 30 embodies the baroque style. The double cornice crowning the chest consists of a convex section which conceals a shallow drawer for storing documents and a flat frieze beneath an elaborate molding. The moldings around the cornice and drawers and between the two main parts of the chest are cut in bold classical outlines. Some are half-round, others are more complex, but all contribute to the grandeur of the piece. The use of inlaid borders and veneers to enliven the surface is characteristic for the period. In its simple elegance and majesty, this chest is particularly representative of the William and Mary style.

Burl walnut veneer produces an emphatic surface treatment, especially when sections are arranged to oppose the grain, creating symmetrical patterns (31). Employed extensively at the beginning of the eighteenth century, this veneer gives a more brilliant effect than the inlays of 30, although veneering is actually less complicated. The burl graining is the natural counterpart of the technique called marquetry, which was used on English furniture. Lacking a frieze, but with the same kind of trumpet-turned legs under a gracefully curving skirt as on 30, this piece offers one of the many variations in high chest design of the William and Mary period.

32

31. *High chest with walnut veneer*

Surface embellishment is an important feature of William and Mary furniture, and a number of different kinds were used. Here (32), the treatment is japanning. Unlike the earlier japanning, where the effect hardly resembles its oriental source, William and Mary japanning much more closely approximates lacquered decoration, both in texture and subject matter. The oriental animals and figures in a landscape were built up in relief with gesso, which was then gilded. The basic shape of the chest is very much like that of 31. The turnings of the legs are simpler, but the outlines of the moldings are similar in proportion, though less complex. A family history traces the chest to its original owner, Benjamin Pickman of Boston and Salem, Massachusetts.

This squat high chest has only one drawer in the lower section instead of the usual three or five, and three front legs rather than four (33). Its japanning is simpler than that of 32, without gesso under the paint—a primitive technique

32. *Japanned high chest* (*opposite*)

33. *Squat high chest*

34. Spice box

used by "country" craftsmen. The schematically rendered decoration represents flowers and birds. The effect is charming—the successful interpretation of a sophisticated design on the level of popular art.

Although the paneled doors of this "spice box" (34) are cut and planed in a design that is usually associated with the 1730s, the trumpet-turned legs, the stretchers, and the hardware are typical of the William and Mary style. It is probably a late piece of the period, dating close to 1730. Miniature chests such as this one, familiar earlier in the colonies (15), were set atop tables and were used to store valuables.

Tables with slate or marble tops have been called "mixing tables," since it is thought that they were used in food preparation, where liquids might damage a wooden surface. This example (35) was made in New England. The slate and the octagonal marquetry frame of the top have been related to documented exports from Danzig. In one article, the marquetry borders were compared to

35. *Slate-topped table*

examples in the Schweizerische National Museum in Zurich. Whatever the origins of the top, it is a prime example of a more complex pattern than those of American tables. The table base, however, is clearly of American manufacture. The lines are much like those of other colonial examples, and all of the woods used—maple, cherry, pine, and birch—are American. The trumpet-turned legs are strengthened by a set of stretchers that intersect each other instead of going around the sides; consequently, a person can sit comfortably with his legs under the table. Dovetailed edges are exposed at the front, a reminder that the piece was constructed by the cabinetmaking technique rather than by joinery. Very likely the dovetails were less visible originally, when the table was stained a darker brown.

In 36, the basic book box has been enlarged and placed on a stand. Although the simple shape suggests a date of about 1680, the dovetails, the arches that compose the skirt, and the design of the turned legs date the piece to the William and Mary period. The slant-top surface was originally intended to be a book rest or writing desk and has an outer edge planed in a classical molding.

36. *Slant-top desk-on-frame*

37. *Looking glass and desk*
(opposite)

The pattern of the turned legs combines two kinds of vases in the heavy proportions that designate a New York rather than a New England origin. The provenance is confirmed by other connections: the desk was found in New York, with a Dutch inscription on it, and the wood is red gumwood, which is native to New York.

This looking glass and desk (37) epitomize the William and Mary style. Elegance is achieved through both form and color, and veneers provide surface patterns that complement the forms. The bold convex molding that frames the mirror and the cut-out crest that crowns it are especially fine. The curve of the molding suggests architectural details of the period, such as fireplace mantels. Equally in the spirit of the best William and Mary design is the intricate classical pattern of the cut-out. The desk served for storage as well as for writing. In this case the part of the desk used for writing is not the slant top but the horizontal surface created when the top is dropped open. The graining of the wood, the bold moldings, and the ball feet are characteristic baroque elements of the style.

Queen Anne Style

1730–1760

Queen Anne is the first distinctively eighteenth-century style of American furniture. It came into fashion about 1730 and thrived until about 1760, when the Chippendale style overshadowed but did not completely replace it. Queen Anne was still popular enough in the 1780s to be included along with Chippendale in a furniture price book issued by a Philadelphia lumber merchant named Lehman. The American Queen Anne style actually postdates the reign of the queen (1702–14), and it includes designs known as English Georgian. The American Queen Anne is characterized by a lightness and restrained elegance that is reminiscent of rococo designs of the Old World, most aptly represented by the curving animal-form leg introduced about 1730. The leg is usually plain, occasionally with shell ornament on the knee, and the foot is either a plain pad, a trifid, or a claw and ball.

Although regional origins can be detected in some earlier work, after about the 1730s each major center developed unique characteristics in furniture manufacture and decoration, and Philadelphia, New York, Newport, and Boston each produced distinctive work with only occasional borrowings between the centers. In Philadelphia, craftsmen were clearly aware of the latest London furniture, and they tended to offer examples with more carved embellishments than cabinetmakers in other cities. Connoisseurs have noted a similarity between stylish Irish work and that of Philadelphia. Whether or not any connection actually existed, Irish emigrants were numerous in the city, and Philadelphia, like Dublin, turned out furniture with heavy proportions and carving that is less finely detailed than London efforts, but nevertheless elegant.

New York cabinetmakers developed a preference for heavy proportions and a minimum of decoration. The New England version was much lighter, varying from the very subdued to the elaborate. Among other features, New England style displayed a sharp edge at the knee of the standard cabriole leg.

The leg from a fine Queen Anne chair is the logical introduction to the style (38a), since it demonstrates the most dramatic aesthetic change. While earlier legs were limited by the capacities of the lathe and the most economical use of

38a. *Cabriole leg, detail of 38*

wooden planks, this leg was conceived of without regard for economy, either of time or material. The curving form is carved from a solid board, but to achieve a graceful line, two additional pieces have been carved and affixed at the top. The carved shell on the knee and the three-point pattern of the foot, called the trifid, are the most elaborate features to be seen on Queen Anne furniture, but they show the restraint typical of the period.

The cabriole leg may characterize the Queen Anne style, but only in the whole chair can we see the delicate balance of classical and exotic features (38). The vase-shaped splat, the scrolls on the splat and back, the shells on the back and legs, the shaping of the stiles, rails, and the seat are classical elements, but the overall design owes its inspiration to oriental models. The

38. *Side chair*

curving back, a predominant feature of the Queen Anne style, is an adaptation of the Chinese-style chair, with its solid wooden frame and straight splat. The foot, the shell design, and the exaggerated curves of the back identify this as a Philadelphia chair.

The armchair is the ideal Queen Anne form. One typical design is 39, a series of curves cut with great skill and sensitivity to take full advantage of beautifully grained mahogany. This armchair is one of the most handsome examples of its kind. An outstanding feature is the richly carved spoon-shaped arm supports. As is typical of many Queen Anne examples, there is almost no relief ornament aside from the scrolls at the ends of the arms and the leaf forms at the front knees. The curves not only add elegance but are proportioned to make the chair look comfortable. The extravagance of the front curves in contrast to the extremely plain rear stump legs indicates that the chair was made in Philadelphia.

39. *Armchair*

40. *Side chair (opposite, left)*

41. *Connecticut side chair (opposite, right)*

This expression of the Queen Anne style (40) could be produced with less time and less effort than 38 or 39. The design is curiously reactionary, with turned stiles, stretchers, and legs, and little carved detail—a mixture of William and Mary and Queen Anne features. The design appears in the advertisement of a chairmaker in the early 1800s, however, and it was no doubt a long-lived standard form for craftsmen producing inexpensive work.

Here is a simple but a more fashionable chair (41). The use of straight stiles and a straight-sided rectangular seat results in a form almost as graceful as the

more elegantly curved Philadelphia chairs. The curves in the bottom of the skirt substitute for the more elaborate sculpted frames of other examples. The design is characteristic of chairs made in Connecticut, where craftsmen simplified the lines of the models. The curving skirt relates to those on William and Mary pieces and is typical of the work of the rural stylist, who chose conservative details that could be executed with less time and expense than the extravagant versions. The turned stretcher resembles that of 40. The needlework of the seat is the original, a fine example of the large-scale patterns employed in eighteenth-century upholstery and drapery. The wool embroidery, crewelwork, follows a conservative floral pattern that resembles seventeenth-century work in both its simple design and its vivid colors.

More refined and stylish needlework is found on this more exuberant chair, another product of Philadelphia (42). The needlework seats of both 41 and 42 are based on East India cotton patterns, which are known in painted as well as

42. *Philadelphia side chair*

43. *Armchair with openwork slat* (*opposite, left*)

44. *Roundabout chair* (*opposite, right*)

printed versions. 41 is closer to early examples, while this one is a freer interpretation of the Indian designs, worked in the subdued color scheme that was introduced in the 1730s. The splat, the shell on the top rail, and the legs of 42 compare with the details of 41, but the seat of 42 has the extra embellishment of the horseshoe shaping of the back.

The openwork splat is usually associated with the Chippendale style rather than the Queen Anne, but it was employed in English models as early as the 1730s, and occasional American examples with the curving Queen Anne back have pierced splats and claw-and-ball feet. This particularly handsome chair (43) reflects the spirit of the gracefully restrained Queen Anne style. The piece is difficult to date, however, since it is not known how soon Americans began to copy English models after they were aware of them.

This corner chair (44), called a roundabout in the eighteenth century, is a form that was often made with a deep skirt to conceal a commode. When the

skirt was shallow, the roundabout was intended to serve as a desk or dressing table chair. This example is particularly fine; all four legs are cut in the cabriole shape and terminate in embellished pad feet. The supports curve dramatically, complementing the elaborate scroll ends of the arms.

Upholstered chairs like 45 were known in the eighteenth century as easy chairs, but are now called wing chairs, after the projecting sides that look as if they could flap. 45 is an outstanding example, still covered with its original fabric. The front of the upholstery is in a pattern that had achieved international popularity in the eighteenth century, a repeating geometric design that is a variation of the flamestitch. The back has been worked in a striking bucolic landscape with sheep, shepherds, deer, and birds set in a series of stylized hills.

45. *Wing chair, front and back*

The trees sprouting from some of the hills look like they were taken from part of a crewelwork hanging. The plain legs terminating in plain pad feet characterize, in their simplicity and grace, one aspect of the Queen Anne style.

49

46. *High chest*

47. *Japanned high chest*

47a. *Detail of angel*
from pediment of 47

After 1730 storage pieces were made with more ambitious classical elements. Prime examples are the high chests, which were often crowned with pediments, a feature that expands the architectural concept of William and Mary pilasters and moldings. Flaming urns at the corners of the pediments, shells that appear to be vestigial niches from classical monuments, and fluted pilasters that flank the drawers and support the pediment are typical of Queen Anne case pieces. Such architectural details were put into an organic context by placing the case on the characteristic cabriole leg. The solid form seems less massive and more intimate. Although the pediment and tall, curving legs made the Queen Anne chest look more impressive than those of the William and Mary period, the basic design remained much the same.

The high chest was meant to be both decorative and useful. The front of 46 is handsomely veneered in walnut, providing a patterned surface like those of the early eighteenth century, but the total effect of the piece is strikingly different. The lean legs, the pilasters on either side of the upper drawers, and the pediment with urn finials lighten the solid proportions of the basic form. Richly carved and gilded shells complement the plainness of the piece.

The form of 47 is essentially the same as that of 46, but because its surface has been japanned it looks more elaborate. The Chinese landscapes and figures have been built up with gesso and gilded. When japanning was first introduced in the seventeenth century, it was rendered in flatter patterns, but most eighteenth-century japanned designs resemble genuine lacquer more

48. *Japanned low chest*

49. *Rhode Island low chest*

50. *Bowlegged japanned high chest*

closely, in choice of subject as well as in the treatment of some elements in relief. Here, the Chinese decoration has been put into a classical context with intricately detailed urns and shells. The rich ornament of the piece has been associated with Boston, and the japanner may have been a Bostonian named Thomas Johnson, known to have been active from about 1730 to 1767.

The low chest (48) was made to complement 47. Very likely they were used together in a bedroom. Low chests often had looking glasses on or over them and may well have served as dressing tables. As is usual, this piece is scaled down from the high chest, but it is decorated in the same way.

The range of design in the Queen Anne style is broad. Although the form of 49 is quite similar to that of 48, the result is much less distinguished. The simple carved shell is the most ostentatious decorative element on this economical version of the eighteenth-century chest. Grace and lightness are imparted by the subtle curving elements in the legs, the skirt, and the top. The wood is cedar, generally found only as a secondary wood, but occasionally encountered in the work of Rhode Island craftsmen.

This japanned high chest (50), which is best described as bowlegged, is a whimsical variant of the standard form. The curious legs are easier to cut and carve than ordinary cabriole legs and may be stronger. The flat top is a more conservative design than the typical pedimented arch, and the half-round strips of molding were more fashionable on William and Mary than on Queen Anne pieces. Although the painted decoration is similar in subject to that of 47, it is applied flat and schematically rather than in relief, and it looks like the chinoiserie of seventeenth-century prints. According to family tradition, this chest can be traced to Connecticut origins as early as the late eighteenth century, but the design looks even earlier. There is a strong possibility that this chest was made before 1750. While the cabinetmaker was conservative in his choice of form and his technique, he was adventurous and ambitious in the subject of his decoration, as were many craftsmen who worked at some distance from a major center.

The drop-leaf table was updated in the Queen Anne period with cabriole legs that replaced the William and Mary turned legs and stretchers (51). The cabriole leg is seen more often with curving leaves rather than rectangular ones. The skirt, visible at the short ends, is cut in curves appropriate to the overall design. This form was made in mahogany, as here, as well as in cherry, maple, and walnut. Some drop-leaf tables have more gracefully curving legs than 51; others have plainer skirts. The heavy proportions of this table suggest a New York origin.

By about 1730 tea-drinking had been transformed from a medicinal practice

51. *Drop-leaf table*

52. *Tea table*

to a ritual of hospitality. For serving tea, small occasional tables were introduced. The tea table was produced in two basic shapes. Both were designed to be used either in front of or between chairs, and each is about the size of a large tray. One is rectangular, supported on four legs; the other is round and rests on a pedestal. Some pedestal tables have tops that can be tilted so that they can be moved against the wall when not in use. 52 is a handsome example of the rectangular type. Although the table has no carving, the moldings around the tray top and bottom of the skirt reflect the abilities of the

55

craftsman. The leg, square in cross-section, with a sharp corner at the knee, is one associated particularly with Newport, Rhode Island. The slipper foot, narrow and terminating in a point, resembles those of the group of furniture that has also been attributed to Newport craftsmen. Oddly enough, another group with the same kind of leg is considered to be Southern, and New Yorkers had their own, thickened version of the design.

Marble-topped tables were one of the most luxurious kinds of furniture made in colonial America and were consequently rare. The tops were ordinarily mined in local quarries and were cut in contours characteristic of mid-eighteenth-century tables. The frames on which they were placed represent some of the finest cabinetmaking technique of the period, sometimes

53. *Marble-topped side table*

54. *Looking glass*

executed by the carvers themselves. Both Philadelphia and New York crafts-men carved the style of claw-and-ball feet seen on 53. The skirt is handsomely grained and neatly curved, with moldings appropriate for the mid-eighteenth century. Although dining rooms were rare even in grand American houses before the Revolution, this table may have served as a side table in a room used mainly for dining. It is an heirloom of the Verplancks, a prominent New York family of the eighteenth century.

The long curving frame of the looking glass (54) was made possible by improvements in glass manufacturing introduced in England and the Conti-nent in the 1700s. Americans preferred the subtly curving line with a fairly simple molded border to pedimented, carved, and gilded forms favored in the Old World. The japanned frame has an ornamental top, a feature more familiar to William and Mary looking glasses. In fact, except for the proportions of this piece, it is very much like examples from the earlier period.

Chippendale Style

1760–1790

While the name "Chippendale" does not adequately define the last American furniture style of the colonial period, it is at least more appropriate than the names of British rulers were for the earlier styles. Many American Chippendale designs were taken from or inspired by the pattern book by Thomas Chippendale, *The Gentleman and Cabinet-Maker's Director,* first published in 1754. Chippendale offered a compendium of the most fashionable designs in London, borrowing freely from the repertory of French rococo ornament. Rococo, a word derived from the French word *rocaille,* meaning "an asymmetrical shell," was applied to the elaborate style that extended the curving, asymmetrical lines of the baroque to a more lightly proportioned fantasy of whimsical and exotic ornaments combined from several sources. Although carved examples are considered most characteristic, the rococo style also includes delicate curving forms with plain surfaces. Chippendale was not the first to adapt this "French" taste to furniture design, but he was nevertheless influential in popularizing it in England and America.

The repertory of ornament found in the *Director* is divided by the author into three categories: the modern or French, the Gothic, and the Chinese. Engravings in the *Director* offer such motifs as shells, scrolls, S-curves, leaves, ribbons, floral patterns, and even Aesop's fables. Carving covered legs, chair backs, and panels of chests. Such sumptuous decor did not end with furniture: houses in both England and America were embellished with rococo decoration on mantels and ceilings.

Curiously enough, Chippendale's publication exerted its strongest influence on American design at the very moment that Robert Adam was introducing a revival of the symmetry and precision of ancient classical design. Neoclassicism, as the new style was called, was all but ignored by the Americans until after the Revolution. Americans, attracted to the new shapes of the rococo in the 1730s, stayed with them until about 1790. Such Queen Anne features as the high chest and the curving cabriole leg with claw-and-ball foot, out of fashion in England by the mid-eighteenth century, were incorporated into the Chippendale style in the colonies.

55. Blockfront chest of drawers

Since the basic forms of furniture remained much as they had been in the Queen Anne period, the dating of Chippendale furniture is based mostly on the amount and style of ornamentation. This system is not completely reliable, however, since plain Queen Anne pieces were probably still offered by cabinetmakers after the Chippendale style had come into vogue and since Americans may have produced elaborately carved work based on English models before Chippendale's *Director* was published. For the most part, though, historians agree that furniture with rococo carved decoration can be assigned to the period after 1760.

The most discussed and admired examples of American Chippendale furniture have little to do with the flamboyant designs in the *Director*. Newport cabinetmakers produced striking designs with an unusual arrangement of three shells carved in high relief, and chests of drawers like 55 represent their best work. The form of the chest, in which the shells characteristically top three sections—two convex flanking one concave—is called a "blockfront." The blockfront design is restrained enough to have been considered Queen Anne style by a few connoisseurs of the 1930s. While there is no immediate English precedent for blocking, it is curiously close to late seventeenth-century designs of desks, dressing tables, and chests with projecting sections by André Charles Boulle, a Parisian cabinetmaker who was better known for his inlay work. Because the antecedents for blocking are so remote, however, the design is usually considered an American phenomenon. Here, the Newport cabinetmaker has shown off his outstanding abilities in the subtle juxtaposition of details, from the handsomely curved moldings and the projecting and receding lines of the blocking to the precise symmetry of the shells and the delicacy of the tiny scrolls on the feet. The light proportions are typical of the mid-eighteenth century and later; the design is similar to the elaborate classical efforts of London cabinetmakers of the 1760s. By reducing the scale, English cabinet-

55a. *Label bearing John Townsend's signature and the date 1765 from drawer of blockfront desk, 55*

makers like William Vile created furniture replete with accurate classical details, such as dentils and leaf borders, that were the miniature version of what had been seen in earlier Palladian furniture of William Kent. Vile's Newport contemporaries retained the proportions but eliminated much of the intricate detail.

55 bears the label of John Townsend, an outstanding Newport cabinetmaker who lived from 1732 to 1809. The Townsends and another Newport family, the Goddards, produced fine furniture throughout the last half of the eighteenth century. Intermarriages created a cohesive group of craftsmen. The Metropolitan Museum collection also includes a tall clock and a card table (60) with John Townsend's label. The clock bears a shell similar to that on the chest, but the table is straight-legged and in what Chippendale called "the Chinese taste."

The triple shell motif, the signature of the Newport cabinetmakers, also appears on a finely executed blockfront desk-and-bookcase (56). The three bookcase doors, an elegant variation of the standard double door, comple-

56. *Blockfront desk-and-bookcase*

57. *Card table attributed to John Goddard*

ment the three sections of the desk. The pattern of two projecting and one concave section crowned with shells is repeated on the slant-top lid and front of the chest. The finely carved urn-shaped finials are another characteristic feature of Newport work. The Newport makers produced many exquisitely made pieces like this one, in which the blocks were cut extravagantly from a solid board rather than from several pieces. Such pieces may not have been in the most current London fashion, but they represent the epitome of fine craftsmanship.

The virtuosity of the Newport cabinetmakers is also displayed in another detail, the distinctive claw-and-ball foot with individual talons cut to stand out from the ball, as on 57. The simple lines of this card table relate to Georgian designs of the 1730s and 1740s. The leaf motif carved in relief on the knee

64

looks incised—almost intaglio—a more subtle effect than typical carving. The table has been attributed to John Goddard, who is known to have made a tea table for Jabez Bowen with similar carving. The undulating line of the skirt of 57 is indeed like those on several Goddard pieces, but the Newport style was probably not exclusive to the Townsends and Goddards. Besides the possibility of other Newport makers, a few makers in Connecticut under Newport influence are known to have used blockfront and shell forms.

The marbletop side or serving table (58) has similar leaf decoration on the legs and the same kind of undercut claws on the feet as 57. The basic form resembles English tables made in the 1720s, but the light proportions and relatively thin contours of the moldings date it to after 1750. Marble-topped tables made for the more affluent interior were relatively rare even in the

58. *Marble-topped side or serving table*

59. *Commode*

Chippendale style. This one was used for communion vessels in a church in the nineteenth and twentieth centuries, but its original function was probably domestic. The ornament on the legs and the character of the claw-and-ball feet are associated with the work of John Goddard.

This commode (59) is a straightforward modification of an English model of what Chippendale called "the French taste." The basic form—a marble-topped chest of drawers on cabriole legs—is more typical of Paris or London products with marquetry and ormolu decoration. The claw-and-ball foot is peculiar to

66

Newport furniture, however, and the plain curving surface in dark-grained wood is typically American. Apparently the maker of the commode was aware of the latest Old World fashion but was careful to adapt his design to suit Newport taste. The use of an adventurous form for an example of Newport work is another instance of American preference for bold design in a traditional context. As with 58, John Goddard has been suggested as the maker of this piece.

This card table (60) in "the Chinese taste" might look at first glance as if it had come out of a London shop, but a label in the drawer bears the name of the Newport craftsman John Townsend and the date 1766. The Chippendale designs Townsend usually followed had delicate lines and complex surface ornament, but his construction of these intricate plans was always sturdy. Although the card table design is "Chinese," the legs are fluted with reeding between the flutes in standard classical fashion—yet another example of the

60. *Card table by John Townsend*

61.
*Bombé
desk-and-
bookcase*

American tradition of combining the new and the familiar. As is typical of Newport style, however, detailing is simplified. Townsend has relied on rich graining, a hatchwork border along the skirt, and nicely carved corner brackets to add grace and formality to an otherwise plain piece.

The bombé, or kettle-shaped, base for chests and desks was an expression of the rococo that appealed to Boston cabinetmakers but seems not to have been especially popular elsewhere in the colonies. The form was known in Continental work as early as the second quarter of the eighteenth century and was used by English cabinetmakers providing furniture for Georgian palaces and fine townhouses. According to tradition, George Washington is supposed to have used this secretary (61) when he was quartered at Craigie House in Cambridge, Massachusetts, in the early days of the Revolution.

An inscription in ink on the bottom of 62 reads: "This desk was maid in the year 1769 Buy Benjn Burnam that sarfed his time in Felledlfay [Philadelphia]."

62.
Desk-and-bookcase by Benjamin Burnham

The writer of this claim is believed to have been Benjamin Burnham of Colchester, Connecticut, a craftsman who could have completed his apprenticeship between about 1750 and 1760. He may have been born either there or in Ipswich, Massachusetts. Little is known about Burnham, but a few pieces of high quality have been attributed to him. Although his training was in Philadelphia, Burnham favored the Connecticut interpretation of blocking and fluted pilasters. The squat ball of the foot, however, is like Philadelphia examples. The inlaid stars on the lid, a convention for Queen Anne pieces of 1730 to 1750, is an old-fashioned element here. Burnham's approach is characteristic of ambitious rural work. He has treated each of the decorative elements with equal emphasis, rather than integrating them into a cohesive composition.

The chest-on-chest was popular in the 1760s. 63, an exquisitely executed piece, may be the work of Thomas Affleck, a Philadelphia cabinetmaker who emigrated from Ireland. The carving could be the work of James Reynolds, who advertised in Philadelphia newspapers as a carver and gilder and a retainer of looking glasses and paints. The handsome decorative detailing appears minimal because of the subtlety with which it was executed. Unlike 62, the design of this chest is so well conceived that the separate elements are noticeable only on close examination.

It was on the high chest, or highboy (64), often with a matching low chest, that Philadelphia cabinetmakers lavished the greatest attention. On the best examples the carved decoration was modeled after elaborate rococo motifs that could be found in Chippendale's *Director,* other books of engravings, or the imported pieces themselves. High chests were a blend of the old and the new, perfect for the colonial patron, whose vision of elegance was colored by his remembrance of affluent Old World homes. The best of the Philadelphia high chests, like this example, have rich rococo carving across the upper area between the scrolls of the pediment and in the lower area on the bottom

63. *Chest-on-chest*

64. *Philadelphia high chest*

71

center drawer as well as the skirt. The moldings and the engaged columns with their floral, leaf, and meander motifs are more classical than rococo. On the other hand, the scroll, ribbon, and leaf ornament between the pediments and on the skirt suggest the lightness and whimsy of the rococo style. The squat appearance of the claw-and-ball feet and the overall richness of the piece are typical of Philadelphia workmanship. The combination of old-fashioned design features with an exuberant display of fine carving and cabinetmaking appealed to Philadelphia's affluent families.

The low chest (65), presumably used as a dressing table, is smaller in scale but otherwise repeats the lower section of 64. Because the forms are matching, they are often thought to have been intended for use in a bedroom. High chests are mentioned in early nineteenth-century descriptions of parlors, however, so there is a strong possibility that they were also used as parlor furniture. Such a handsome piece as this low chest deserves to have been placed in a room where it could be seen by many.

Carving on Philadelphia furniture of the Chippendale era was often the work of a specialist. Here (66) the carver has found inspiration in a design for a chimney piece published in *A New Book of Ornaments* by Thomas Johnson Carver (London, 1762). Birds are the major elements in a complex pattern of leaves, flowers, and scrolls. Fables were one of the more popular subjects for rococo decoration, and Chippendale illustrated several Aesop fables that were in the same decorative spirit as this panel.

The high chest that bears the panel is now known as the "Pompadour highboy," after the female bust topping it, which may be a likeness of the famous French courtier. The bust has been so stylized that identification can be only speculative, but busts of celebrities were popular as embellishments for furniture and for pediments over doorways. The pierced foliate pattern between the scrolls of the pediment and the fretwork on the cornices of both sections are carved to suggest the vitality of rococo without an excess of

65. *Low chest*

66. *"Pompadour highboy"*

67. *Tilt-top table*

ornamentation. The narrow border of molding that frames the drawers is a detail that is also found on contemporary English cabinetwork. Here, again, Philadelphia craftsmanship is shown at its best.

The tilt-top circular table (67) was made for serving tea. Here, a small cage-shaped support was included to make it possible to rotate the top as well as to tip it. The carved decoration is typical of Philadelphia work. The carved ornament of the baluster base is classically inspired, but the scalloped top is rococo.

The rectangular tea table (68) has the characteristic straight legs of the "Chinese taste" illustrated in Chippendale's book. The molded, curving profile of the legs is a suitable complement to the plain skirt. The stretchers meet in the center in what appears to be the outline of a pagoda, but their curving scroll pattern is the single French rococo element. Casters make the table mobile, a practical note rarely encountered on American Chippendale furniture. The plain gallery around the top and the heaviness of the stretchers suggest this is a work from one of the smaller American cities, and, confirming this, the piece has indeed been traced to Portsmouth, New Hampshire.

68.
Tea table

Card tables were known before 1760, but Chippendale and later examples are more common. This version of the straight-legged card table (69), with its gadrooning, curving sides, a band of beading along the legs, and the flamboyant drawerpulls is more ornate than 60. The furniture maker has combined French and Chinese motifs illustrated in the *Director*. The high relief of the carving, which provides dramatic contrasts of light and shadow, marks the table as a product of Philadelphia.

Another card table (70) reflects a more restrained, but equally characteristic American approach. The turret ends and broad cabriole legs carved in a leaf-and-scroll pattern compare more closely to London examples of the 1730s than those of the 1750s. The distinguishing factor is the character of the carving. Here, it is thicker and bolder than on contemporary London pieces, and the overall effect of grace and elegance is achieved without frills.

69. *Philadelphia card table*

70. *New York card table*

71. *New York card table with five legs*

Collectors today prize New York card tables of the Chippendale period more than those of any other center, although other forms made in New York are in less demand. An explanation for their popularity can be found in an examination of this example (71). The overall design is bold and rich. Typical of New York, it seems sturdier than the Philadelphia examples. It has five legs instead of four to give support to the top when it is opened. The rear talon of the claw-and-ball foot is straight, and the knuckles of the front talons appear to be the points of a square, a treatment that adds to the appearance of strength. Richly detailed carving on the legs serves as a foil for the bolder and simpler border of gadrooning along the curving skirt.

The character of the decoration of this marble-topped side table (72) is quite different from that of 58, although they were made at about the same time. Compared to the most elaborate Chippendale furniture, like 73, both 58 and 72 are conservative, but of the two 72 is more clearly in the rococo spirit. The Philadelphia maker followed the local practice of adorning a curving form with shells. Although those on the knees of the cabriole legs are the type associated with the Queen Anne style, the delicately articulated carving of the center shell is more elaborate—a clearly Chippendale detail. The claw-and-ball feet

72. *Marble-topped side table*

73. *Cadwalader table*

are rather squat with talons rendered in more detail than those by craftsmen from New York or Newport.

73 is possibly the most lavishly carved American table known. It was made in Philadelphia for the Cadwaladers, a prominent family whose household was filled with splendid, sumptously decorated furniture. The table may well have been inspired by an engraving from the Chippendale *Director* or another popular pattern book. The carving is more solid and less intricate than on English work in the same style, particularly in the curves of the legs and skirts. Nonetheless, the scrolls and the added ribbon and foliate motifs are applied with the seeming abandon typical of the rococo, only mildly tempered to suit American taste.

Gilt frames, unusual on English looking glasses, are especially rare on

74. *Looking glass*

75. *Side chair*

76. *Ladderback side chair*

American examples. Like 73, 74 is carved in the full rococo style, and the wood almost appears to embellish the glass rather than frame it. The thickness of detail serves to distinguish the piece from English work, which is more delicate and more whimsical.

The splat and yoke-shaped rail of this chair (75) were inspired by a Chippendale design, but the overall lines of the back resemble English models of the 1740s. A closer examination reveals the use of an overall pattern of carving on the back found at its best in the work of Philadelphia craftsmen. The

80

Philadelphia attribution is confirmed by other details: one is the claw-and-ball foot, which resembles those on the marble-topped table (72). Besides marking the chair as Philadelphian, the feet also distinguish it as American, since claw-and-ball feet were out of fashion in London and were not even included in the *Director*.

The Chippendale ladderback design (76) was produced even after 1780, when the style itself was no longer in fashion. Daniel Trotter, a Philadelphia craftsman, to whom this chair is attributed, continued producing this type in

77. *Boston side chair*

the 1790s. Whether or not it was made during the actual Chippendale period, the basic form is a variation of the yoke-backed, straight-legged chair, a familiar Chippendale pattern. The splats and rails are well executed, and the plain legs are finished neatly at the corners. The delicacy and crispness of the rosette and leaf motifs suggest the piece may have been executed after the Revolution.

Elegantly detailed American chairs vary in proportion and in their dependence upon English models. Here (77), the elegance is the result of tempering London inspiration with a delicacy that appealed to Boston cabinetmakers.

82

The design is from *The Cabinet and Chairmaker's Real Friend and Companion*, by Robert Manwaring, who, like Chippendale, was a cabinetmaker-author, but the interpretation is distinctively Bostonian. The sparing use of wood for the back splat is characteristic of the city, and in the Boston version of the claw-and-ball foot, the talons grasp the ball tightly, making the curve of the leg more dramatic. The leaf carving on the legs is deep—another detail that was old-fashioned but typical of the American approach to design.

The legs of the small settee (78) are similar to those of 78, but the carved scroll pattern on the knees is more complex than the leaf design in the chair. The lightness and delicacy of the form is characteristic of fine Boston crafts-manship. The full-blown rococo is once again combined with more restrained earlier designs.

78. *Settee*

The wing chair is another conservative form produced in the Chippendale era. The top rail is often made to curve in a lighter outline in the 1760s, as on the example here (79), and the arms are made as delicate as possible. The legs are like those of the Boston chair (77), strengthened by stretchers, a dated but practical addition favored by many New England chair makers.

More in keeping with the fashions of the 1760s and later is the armchair with upholstered seat and back and plain wooden arms (80). The straight legs, which are decorated with a fleur-de-lis carved in relief, derive from the *Director*. The form of the chair is one that was most favored in Philadelphia. Among examples of this type still surviving, the best known are those made for Governor John Penn, who commissioned the finest furniture from the foremost Philadelphia cabinetmakers. One of these makers, Thomas Affleck, was probably the maker of this chair. Affleck and his fellow cabinetmakers had managed to produce American furniture that was much closer to London design than the simple work of their seventeenth-century predecessors. Nevertheless, American furniture produced on the eve of the Revolution, like this armchair, was as distinctive in its way as that of the joiners in the early settlements.

79. *Wing chair*

80. *Upholstered armchair.*
(see page 86)

84

Checklist

Seventeenth-century, or Pilgrim, Style

P. 3 Parlor of the Thomas Hart house, Ipswich, Massachusetts. About 1640. 36.127, Munsey Fund, 1936

1 Armchair
New York, 1670–90
Ash
H. 39½ x W. 24 x D. 17 in.
41.111, Rogers Fund, 1941

2 Armchair
New England, 1650–1700
Pine and ash
H. 42 x W. 24 x D. 15½ in.
10.125.235, Gift of Mrs. Russell Sage, 1909

3 Wainscot armchair
New England, 1680–1700
White oak
H. 43 x W. 24⅜ x D. 24⅜ in.
10.88, Gift of Mrs. Russell Sage, 1909

4 Chair-table
Massachusetts, 1675–1700
White oak and pine
H. seat 19½, table top L. 53 x W. 24 in.
10.125.697, Gift of Mrs. Russell Sage, 1909

5 Upholstered chair
Probably Connecticut, 1650–75
Maple and oak
H. 37 x W. 20½ x D. 17½ in.
52.77.51, Bequest of Mrs. J. Insley Blair, 1952

6 Chest
Attributed to Thomas Dennis, Ipswich, Massachusetts, 1680–1700
Oak
H. 29¾ x W. 48 x D. 21⅜ in.
10.125.685, Gift of Mrs. Russell Sage, 1909

7 Chest
Massachusetts (Long Island family history), 1640–80
Oak and chestnut
H. 24½ x W. 47½ x D. 20¼ in.
31.30, The Sylmaris Collection, Gift of George Coe Graves, 1931

8 Chest with two drawers
Wethersfield area, Connecticut, 1675–1705
Oak, pine, cedar, and maple
H. 39⅞ x W. 48 x D. 21¼ in.
66.190.1, Gift of Mrs. J. Woodhull Overton, 1966

9 Chest
Probably Hadley, Massachusetts, 1700–10
Oak and pine
H. 42 x W. 45 x D. 18½ in.
48.158.9, Gift of Mrs. J. Insley Blair, 1948

10 Chest with drawer
Wethersfield area, Connecticut, 1705
Painted oak and pine
H. 33 x W. 48¾ x D. 20½ in.
10.125.29, Gift of Mrs. Russell Sage, 1909

11 Chest of drawers
Massachusetts, 1680–1700
Painted oak and pine
H. 40 x W. 40½ x D. 22⅛ in.
48.158.11, Gift of Mrs. J. Insley Blair, 1948

12 Court cupboard
Connecticut, about 1700
Oak
H. 57¾ x W. 44¼ x D. 21¾ in.
53.197.1, Gift of Mrs. J. Woodhull Overton in memory of Mrs. J. Insley Blair, 1953

13 Press cupboard
New Haven Colony, Connecticut, 1650–80
Oak
H. 56¾ x W. 49½ x D. 21 in.
10.125.703, Gift of Mrs. Russell Sage, 1909

14 Press cupboard
Plymouth County, Massachusetts, 1670–90
Oak, pine, cedar, and maple
H. 56 x W. 49¾ x D. 23 in.
50.20.3, Gift of Mrs. J. Insley Blair, 1950

15 Cabinet (jewel or spice box)
Massachusetts, dated 1679
Oak, pine, walnut, and maple
H. 18 x W. 17 x D. 10 in.
10.125.168, Gift of Mrs. Russell Sage, 1909

16 Trestle table
New England, 1650
Pine and oak
H. 36 x W. 146½ x D. 24 in.
10.125.701, Gift of Mrs. Russell Sage, 1909

17 Gateleg folding table
Essex County, Massachusetts, 1675–1700
Painted oak and maple
H. 27 x Diam. of top 36 in.
51.12.1, Gift of Mrs. J. Insley Blair, 1951

18 Table
Massachusetts, late seventeenth century
Oak, pine, maple, and ash
H. 29½ x W. 41½ x D. 39½ in.
49.155.1, Gift of Mrs. J. Insley Blair, 1949

19 Joint stool
1650–75
Maple
H. 23½ x W. 18 x D. 11 in.
10.125.330, Gift of Mrs. Russell Sage, 1909

20 Cradle
Seventeenth century
White oak
H. 23½ x L. 37 in.
10.125.672, Gift of Mrs. Russell Sage, 1909

21 Box-on-frame with drawer
Eastern Massachusetts, about 1675
Oak, pine, poplar, and maple
H. 35⅝ x W. 26½ x D. 18⅛ in.
69.209, Gift of Mrs. J. Woodhull Overton, 1969

William and Mary Style
1690–1730
P. 23 Wentworth House, Portsmouth, New
Hampshire. About 1710. 26.290, Sage Fund,
1926

22 Armchair
Probably New England, 1690–1700
Oak (seat and frame), maple, and beech
H. 50½ x W. 25 x D. 15¾ in.
30.120.73, Gift of George Coe Graves, The
Sylmaris Collection, 1930

23 Side chair
Probably New York, 1700–20
Red maple and oak
H. 48 x W. 18 x D. 15 in.
52.77.58, Bequest of Mrs. J. Insley Blair, 1952

24 Side chair
Probably New England, about 1700
Maple
H. 47⅜ x W. 21 x D. 15¾ in.
52.195.8, Gift of Mrs. Screven Lorillard, 1952

25 Butterfly table
New England, 1700–25
Maple
H. 25⅝ x W. 42½ x D. 34½ in.
52.77.54, Bequest of Mrs. J. Insley Blair, 1952

26 Table
Massachusetts, 1700–25
Maple and oak
H. 27 x W. 31½ x 26⅝ in.
52.195.4, Gift of Mrs. Screven Lorillard, 1952

27 Gateleg table
New England, 1700–25
Walnut and maple (?)
H. 25½ x Diam. of top 32½ in.
52.77.57, Bequest of Mrs. J. Insley Blair, 1952

28 Gateleg table
Probably New England, 1675–1700
Maple
H. 28½ x W. 54½ x D. 48½ in.
10.125.133, Gift of Mrs. Russell Sage, 1909

29 Chest with drawer
Guilford, Connecticut, 1700–35
Painted pine
H. 33¼ x W. 46 x D. 19 in.
45.78.4, Gift of Mrs. J. Insley Blair, 1945

30 High chest
New England, early eighteenth century
Walnut, walnut veneer, and pine
H. 65 x W. 37½ x D. 22 in.
50.228.2, Gift of Mrs. J. Insley Blair, 1950

31 High chest
New England, about 1700
Walnut veneer, maple, and pine
H. 62½ x W. (top) 35¼, W. (base) 39¼ x D. 21¾ in.
52.195.2a,b, Gift of Mrs. Screven Lorillard, 1952

32 High chest
Massachusetts, about 1730
Japanned maple and white pine
H. 62½ x W. 39½ x D. 21¼ in.
40.37.3, Purchase, Joseph Pulitzer Bequest, 1940

33 High chest
New England, 1710–25
Japanned pine
H. 52 x W. 39½ x D. 21¾ in.
10.125.709, Gift of Mrs. Russell Sage, 1909

34 Cabinet (spice box)
Pennsylvania, about 1730
Walnut and pine
H. 28⅞ x W. 16½ in.
11.183, Gift of Mrs. Fanny Avery Welcher, 1911

35 Slate-topped table
New England, 1710–30
Maple (legs), cherry (stretchers), pine (back), birch (front and sides), various European woods (top), and slate
H. 28½ x W. 35⅛ x D. 25 in.
30.120.56, The Sylmaris Collection, Gift of George Coe Graves, 1930

36 Slant-top desk-on-frame
New York, about 1700
Red gumwood
H. 35¼ x W. 33¾ x D. 24 in.
44.47, Rogers Fund, 1944

37 Looking glass
New England, 1690–1710
Walnut veneer and pine
H. 35⅛ x W. 23⅞ in.
52.195.1, Gift of Mrs. Screven Lorillard, 1952

Slant-top desk
Massachusetts, 1700–20
Burled ash veneer, walnut (bandings); oak, pine, and walnut casings
H. 40 x W. 30 x D. 18½ in.
10.125.75, Gift of Mrs. Russell Sage, 1909

Queen Anne Style,
1730–1760

P. 40 Parlor of the Metcalf-Bowler House, Portsmouth, Rhode Island. Before 1763.
16.120, Purchase, Rogers Fund, 1916

38 Side chair
Philadelphia, 1725–50
Walnut
H. 41⅝ x W. 21 x D. 17 in.
25.115.9, Rogers Fund, 1925

39 Armchair
Philadelphia, 1740–60
Walnut
H. 41 x W. 32 x D. 18½ in.
25.115.36, Rogers Fund, 1925

40 Side chair
New York, 1730–80
Painted maple
H. 40¾ x W. 20 x D. 15¾ in.
33.121.2, Rogers Fund, 1933

41 Side chair
Connecticut, 1725–40
Maple
H. $43\frac{1}{4}$ x W. $21\frac{1}{2}$ x D. 17 in.
46.194.1, Gift of Mrs. J. Insley Blair, 1946

42 Side chair
Philadelphia, 1725–50
Mahogany
H. $41\frac{5}{8}$ x W. 21 x D. 17 in.
25.115.5, Rogers Fund, 1925

43 Armchair
Philadelphia, about 1760
Mahogany and elm
H. $43\frac{1}{2}$ x W. 33 x D. $17\frac{1}{2}$ in.
25.115.18, Rogers Fund, 1925

44 Corner or roundabout chair
Philadelphia, 1725–50
Walnut
H. $30\frac{3}{4}$ x W. $27\frac{1}{2}$ x D. $24\frac{1}{2}$ in.
25.115.15, Rogers Fund, 1925

45 Wing chair
New England, about 1725
Walnut and maple
H. $46\frac{3}{4}$ x W. $31\frac{1}{2}$ in.
50.228.3, Gift of Mrs. J. Insley Blair, 1950

46 High chest
New England, 1725–50
Burl walnut veneer and white pine
H. $89\frac{1}{2}$ x W. 43 x D. 22 in.
10.125.62a,b, Gift of Mrs. Russell Sage, 1909

47 High chest
Boston, Massachusetts, 1730–50
Maple and white pine
H. $85\frac{1}{4}$ x W. $40\frac{1}{2}$ x D. 22 in.
40.37.1, Purchase, Joseph Pulitzer Bequest, 1940

48 Low chest
Boston, Massachusetts, 1730–50
Japanned maple and pine
H. 30 x W. $33\frac{1}{2}$ x D. $20\frac{3}{4}$ in.
40.37.2, Purchase, Joseph Pulitzer Bequest, 1940

49 Low chest
Rhode Island, 1725–50
Cedar
H. $30\frac{1}{2}$ x W. 34 x D. $22\frac{5}{8}$ in.
50.145.359, Bequest of Mary Stillman Harkness, 1950

50 High chest
Windsor area, Connecticut, about 1740
Japanned maple and pine
H. $62\frac{1}{8}$ x W. 35 x D. $20\frac{1}{2}$ in.
46.194.5a,b, Gift of Mrs. J. Insley Blair, 1946

51 Drop-leaf table
New York, about 1740
Mahogany
H. $27\frac{1}{2}$ x W. 25 x D. $12\frac{1}{2}$ in.
34.146, Rogers Fund, 1934

52 Tea table
Newport, Rhode Island, about 1740
Mahogany
H. $26\frac{1}{4}$ x W. $29\frac{1}{2}$ x D. $19\frac{1}{2}$ in.
25.115.27, Rogers Fund, 1925

53 Side table
New York, 1725–50
Mahogany and marble
H. $29\frac{1}{8}$ x W. 40 x D. $24\frac{1}{4}$ in.
39.184.10, Gift of James Delancey Verplanck,
    and John Bayard Rodgers Verplanck, 1939

54 Looking glass
Boston, Massachusetts, 1725–50
Japanned white pine
H. $57\frac{3}{4}$ x W. $19\frac{1}{4}$ in.
40.37.4, Purchase, Joseph Pulitzer Bequest, 1940

Chippendale Style,
1760–1790

P. 58 Room from Powel House, Philadelphia,
    Pennsylvania. 1768. 18.87.1–4, The Rogers
    Fund, 1918

55 Chest of drawers

John Townsend, Newport, Rhode Island, labeled and dated 1765

Mahogany, tulip poplar (?), and white pine (?)

H. 34¼ x W. 36¾ x D. 19 in.

27.57.1, Rogers Fund, 1927

56 Desk-and-bookcase

Attributed to John Goddard, Newport, Rhode Island, 1760–65

Mahogany and other woods

H. 99½ x W. 44½ x D. 13½ in.

15.21.2, Rogers Fund, 1915

57 Card table

Attributed to John Goddard, Newport, Rhode Island, 1760–65

Mahogany, maple, chestnut, and pine

H. 27¾ x W. 33¼ x D. 16½ in.

67.114.1, The Friends of the American Wing Fund, 1967

58 Table

Attributed to John Goddard, Newport, Rhode Island, 1760–70

Mahogany, mahogany veneer, maple, and marble

H. 28½ x W. 49½ x D. 16⅝ in.

62.138a,b, Bequest of Vincent D. Andrus, 1962

59 Commode

Attributed to John Goddard, Newport, Rhode Island, about 1760

Mahogany, chestnut, marble, and brass

H. 34⅜ x W. 36½ x D. 21½ in.

1972.130, Purchase, Emily C. Chadbourne Bequest; Gifts of Mrs. J. Amory Haskell and Mrs. Russell Sage; and The Sylmaris Collection, Gift of George Coe Graves, by exchange, 1972

60 Card table

John Townsend, Newport, Rhode Island, labeled and dated 1766

Mahogany and other woods

H. 27¼ x W. 37⅞ x D. 16⅞ in.

27.161, Purchase, Egleston Fund, 1927

61 Desk-and-bookcase

Massachusetts, 1760–75

Mahogany and other woods

H. 100 x W. 45 x D. 25 in.

John Stewart Kennedy Fund, 1918

62 Desk

Benjamin Burnham, Colchester, Connecticut, inscribed and dated 1769

Cherry

H. 49¾ x W. 44¼ x D. 24¼ in.

18.110.58, John Stewart Kennedy Fund, 1918

63 Chest-on-chest

Probably by Thomas Affleck, cabinetmaker, and James Reynolds, carver; Philadelphia, about 1770

Mahogany and other woods

H. 97 x W. 45 x D. 24⅛ in.

1975.91, Purchase, Friends of the American Wing and Rogers Fund; Virginia Groomes Gift in memory of Mary W. Groomes; J. Aron & Co., Inc., Mr. and Mrs. Fredrick M. Danziger and Hermann Merkin Gifts, 1975

64 High chest

Philadelphia, 1760–80

Mahogany, poplar (?), and cedar (?)

H. 89¼ x W. 45 x D. 24 in.

18.110.6, John Stewart Kennedy Fund, 1918

65 Low chest

Philadelphia, 1760–80

Mahogany, poplar (?), and cedar (?)

H. 31¾ x W 33¾ x D. 21⅛ in.

18.110.7, John Stewart Kennedy Fund, 1918

66 High chest

Philadelphia, about 1765

Cuban mahogany, poplar, and cedar

H. 91½ x W. 46¾ x D. 24¼ in.

18.110.4, John Stewart Kennedy Fund, 1918

67 Tilt-top table

Philadelphia, 1760–75

Mahogany

H. 29 x Diam. of top 37 in.

18.110.13, John Stewart Kennedy Fund, 1918

68 Tea table
Portsmouth, New Hampshire, about 1770
Mahogany and maple
H. 28¼ x W. 35 x D. 23½ in.
61.42, Purchase, Mrs. Emily Crane Chadbourne
Gift, 1961

69 Card table
Philadelphia, about 1760–75
Mahogany and oak
H. 27¾ x W. 34¾ x D. 34⅛ in.
18.110.10, John Stewart Kennedy Fund, 1918

70 Card table
New York, about 1770
Mahogany
H. 28¾ x W. 32¾ in.
25.115.33, Rogers Fund, 1925

71 Card table
New York, 1760–70
Mahogany and leather
H. 27 x W. 34 x D. 33¼ in.
47.35, Purchase, Joseph Pulitzer Bequest, 1947

72 Side table
Philadelphia, about 1770
Mahogany and marble
H. 30½ x W. 50 x D. 26 in.
61.84, Purchase, The Sylmaris Collection, Gift
of George Coe Graves; Gift of Mrs. Russell
Sage; Funds from Various Donors, and
Rogers Fund, 1961

73 Side table
Philadelphia, about 1765
Mahogany and other woods
H. 32¾ x W. 48¼ x D. 23⅛ in.
18.110.27, John Stewart Kennedy Fund, 1918

74 Looking glass
Philadelphia, about 1765
Pine and gilt
H. 53½ x W. 30¾ in.
35.22, Rogers Fund, 1935

75 Side chair
Philadelphia, 1750–75
Mahogany
H. 41½ x W. 23½ x D. 18 in.
30.120.58, The Sylmaris Collection, Gift of
George Coe Graves, 1930

76 Side chair
Probably Daniel Trotter, Philadelphia, 1780–90
Mahogany
H. 38½ x W. 22 x D. 17½ in.
44.109.2, Rogers Fund, 1944

77 Side chair
Boston or Salem, 1765–70
Mahogany
H. 38⅝ x W. 23½ x D. 17½ in.
39.88.2, Gift of Mrs. Paul Moore, 1939

78 Settee
New England, about 1750–75
Mahogany (front legs) and curly maple (back
legs)
H. 36¾ x W. 58½ x D. 22½ in.
30.120.59, The Sylmaris Collection, Gift of
George Coe Graves, 1930

79 Wing chair
Massachusetts, about 1750–90
Mahogany, red maple, and eastern white pine
H. 47½ x W. 38 x D. 28 in.
67.114.2, The Friends of the American Wing
Fund, 1967

80 Armchair
Attributed to Thomas Affleck, Philadelphia,
about 1770
Mahogany
H. 42⅞ x W. 28¼ x D. 24¼ in.
59.154, Purchase, Sage Fund; The Sylmaris Collection, Gift of George Coe Graves; Robert
G. Goelet Gift; and Funds from Various Donors, 1959

Bibliography

Comstock, Helen. *American Furniture*. New York: 1962

Comstock, Helen. *Concise Encyclopedia of American Antiques*. New York: 1958

Davidson, Marshall, ed. *The American Heritage History of Colonial Antiques.* New York: 1967

Downs, Joseph. *American Furniture in the Henry Francis du Pont Winterthur Museum*. New York: 1952

Kirk, John T. *Early American Furniture*. New York: 1970

Randall, Richard. *American Furniture in the Museum of Fine Arts, Boston*. Boston: 1965